Fifty-Cent Cal

by Tanner Gay
illustrations by Regan Dunnick

Harcourt Brace & Company

Orlando Atlanta Austin Boston San Francisco Chicago Dallas New York Toronto London

Cal had one wish—to have a real mitt to catch with. But mitts cost a lot! Cal knew that wishing wouldn't help.

"My only chance to get some cash is to work for it," thought Cal. "I have to look for jobs."

Just then, Mrs. Ponce said, "Cal, you look as if you're in a trance!"

Cal glanced at Mrs. Ponce. "Do you know of any jobs I can do for cash?"

Mrs. Ponce winced. "You can take this bag for me. I'll give you fifty cents."

Cal started to collect cash right then!

Later, Cal was talking to his family.

"You only have fifty cents?" said his brother Vince.

"It's fifty cents more than I had before," said Cal.

"Cal is right," said Mom.
"Collecting cash is no cinch.
Good luck, Cal!"

People soon heard of the boy who was willing to do jobs for fifty cents. They started calling him Fifty-Cent Cal.

For fifty cents, Cal helped Mrs. Capp catch her dog, Lance. Lance was prancing in wet cement!

Cal helped Mr. Spence plant lettuce for fifty cents—cash. Mrs. Vance gave Cal fifty cents for helping her get a cab.

Cal fed Alice Tan's cat, Cecil, when Alice went to France. He got fifty cents every day for ten days!

Cal helped Mr. Cobb fix his fence. Fifty cents more. Then Cal helped Mr. Cobb take a cot up to his attic. Another fifty cents.

And can you believe Cal got fifty cents for showing Alice Tan a new dance! Alice had Cal dancing and prancing!

Vince laughed. "Cal, you'll never live like a prince working for fifty cents!"

Cal laughed. "Vince, I don't want a palace! I want a mitt."

Cal put away every fifty cents. It took a while, but at last Cal had enough cash to buy the mitt.

Vince hasn't laughed at Cal since then. Cal still takes jobs when he can. Sometimes he gets more than fifty cents now!